DCPL0000135849

 D1756539

𝑅𝐴

Items should be returned on or before the last date shown below. Items not already requested by other borrowers may be renewed in person, in writing or by telephone. To renew, please quote the number on the barcode label. To renew online a PIN is required. This can be requested at your local library.
Renew online @ **www.dublincitypubliclibraries.ie**
Fines charged for overdue items will include postage incurred in recovery. Damage to or loss of items will be charged to the borrower.

Leabharlanna Poiblí Chathair Bhaile Átha Cliath
Dublin City Public Libraries

Dublin City
Baile Átha Cliath

Coolock Branch Tel: 8477781

Date Due	Date Due	Date Due
10. 08.	- 9 MAR 2016	
08. 01. 10.		
04. 05. 10.		
02 OCT 13		

EXPLORING
IRISH CASTLES

PAT DARGAN

NONSUCH

The assistance of the Dublin Institute of Technology in this production is gratefully acknowledged.

By the author of

EXPLORING GEORGIAN DUBLIN

First published 2009

Nonsuch Publishing
119 Lower Baggot Street
Dublin 2, Ireland
www.nonsuchireland.com

© Pat Dargan, 2009

The right of Pat Dargan to be identified as the Author
of this work has been asserted in accordance with the
Copyrights, Designs and Patents Act 1988.

All rights reserved. No part of this book may be reprinted
or reproduced or utilised in any form or by any electronic,
mechanical or other means, now known or hereafter invented,
including photocopying and recording, or in any information
storage or retrieval system, without the permission in writing
from the Publishers.
British Library Cataloguing in Publication Data.
A catalogue record for this book is available from the British Library.

ISBN 978 1 84588 948 7

Typesetting and origination by The History Press
Printed in Great Britain

CONTENTS

GLOSSARY OF TERMS

Arch: A curved head that spans an opening, built with wedge-shaped masonry.

Architrave: The decorated frame around a doorway or window.

Bailey: A castle courtyard or bawn.

Barrel Vault: A vault with a semi-circular roof.

Batter: A pronounced outward slope at the base of a wall.

Bartizan: A small overhanging defensive wall-chamber located in a corner position, with a hole in a floor used to drop missiles on attackers below.

Bawn: A castle courtyard or bailey.

Column: A circular pillar.

Corbel: A stone projecting outwards from a wall often used to support a beam or floor.

Crenellation: A stepped defensive parapet at the top of a wall.

Crow-stepped: The stepped top of a gable wall.

Curtain Wall: A defensive wall surrounding a castle bailey.

Drawbridge: A wooden bridge spanning a castle moat, which can be pulled upwards.

Drum Tower: Circular tower.

Elevation: The façade, or the front, back and sides of a building.

Embrasure: Alcove in wall on inner face of loop or window.

Finial: A tall slim pencil-like decoration, usually on a roof.

Gable: The end wall of a building where the upper portion is triangular in shape.

Garderobe: A medieval privy or W.C.

Gatehouse: A small building or tower that defends the entrance to a castle.

Great Hall: A large well-lit room used for dining and entertaining.

Hall House: Small double-storey castle of the late medieval period.

Hood Moulding: Projecting moulding at top of window or doorway.

Keep: A strong freestanding tower within a castle.

Loop: A tall slender vertical window-opening that allowed a bowman fire on attackers.

Machicolation: A small overhanging defensive wall-chamber with a hole in the floor used to drop missiles on attackers below.

Moat: An artificial dry or water channel surrounding a castle.

Motte: An artificial mound, topped with a wooden building and palisade used as a temporary castle.

Motte-and-Bailey: A pair of joined mounds, topped with a wooden building surrounded by a palisade, used as a temporary castle.

Mullion: Vertical upright between window panes.

Murder Hole: A hole in a ceiling through which attacking fire could be directed downwards from the floor above.

Musket Loop: Small circular loop through which musket fire could be directed.

Palisade: A high fence constructed of wooden stakes.

Parapet: A low protective wall at roof level.

Portcullis: A wooden frame, capable of being raised and lowered, that protects a gateway.

Tower House: A small castle in the form of a single tower.

Transom: Horizontal crosspiece between window panes.

Turret: A small projecting circular tower.

Vault: A stone arch forming a roof or ceiling.

Wall Walk: A walking space along the top of a wall.

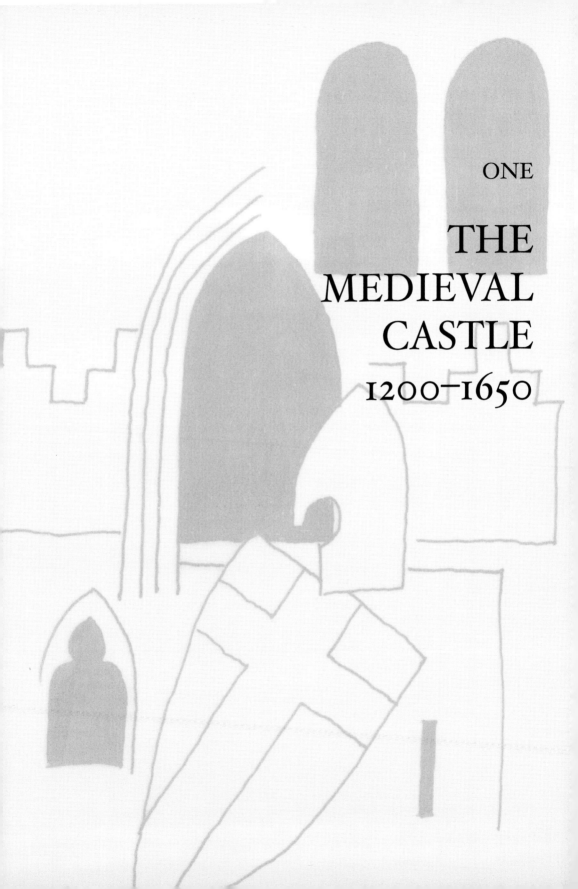

ONE

THE
MEDIEVAL
CASTLE
1200–1650

INTRODUCTION

The visitor to Ireland cannot but be impressed by the number of castles that lie scattered across the landscape. At first it may seem as if all these structures are very similar in terms of their layout and shape. This is not the case, however, as Irish castles fall into a range of different types in regard to their layout, shape, scale, ownership, and construction date.

Few Irish castles can match the complexity and impressiveness of other European examples, such as Dover and Caernarfon castles in Britain, or Banos de la Encina and the Alhambra castles in Spain. Nevertheless, what Irish castles lack in size, they more than make up for in number, as there is scarcely a parish in the land that cannot boast the remains of at least one castle. No recent count of Irish castles has been completed, but it is generally agreed that the number exceeds 3,000. These range in size and complexity, from the large-scale thirteenth-century castles at Trim and Limerick, to the smaller fifteenth-century tower houses at Clara in County Kilkenny and Newtown in County Clare.

THE CASTLE

A castle can be defined as a large stone-built structure that was erected in medieval and post-medieval times for both military and residential purposes. Such structures did not appear in Ireland until the early thirteenth century, during which the Anglo-Normans overran the country and launched a programme of castle building to help them secure their newly conquered lands. Following this, subsequent waves of castle building were launched as later colonists sought to secure their territorial possessions. For this reason, Irish castle building can be classified into four broad historic periods: the Anglo–Norman castles of the thirteenth and fourteenth centuries, tower houses of the fifteenth and sixteenth centuries, and finally fortified houses and Plantation castles of the seventeenth century. Before looking at the development of individual examples, however, it is worth looking at the structural components common to most Irish castles.

LAYOUT

The majority of Irish castles are made up of three principal elements: a keep, a bailey, and a curtain wall. First, the castle had a main tower or keep, usually several storeys high. This was the residential quarter of the castle and it was here that the owner and his family lived. Thus, it contained a range of domestic accommodation including living, sleeping and administration rooms, although it is worth bearing in mind that comfort was not high in the agenda of the castle builders. Secondly, the keep was surrounded by an open courtyard, or bailey. Thirdly, the bailey was enclosed by a protective (or curtain) wall that often included a gatehouse building and a sequence of wall towers; the latter was spaced at regular intervals around the wall circuit, particularly at the corners. All of this meant that that any attacker had to overcome three

Leabharlanna Poibli Chathair Bhaile Átha Cliath
Dublin City Public Libraries

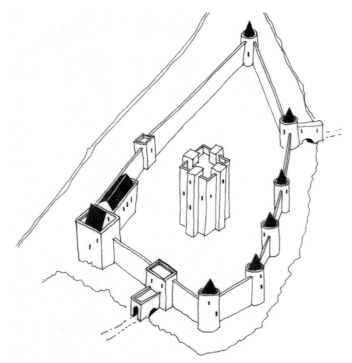

Fig. 1: Conjectural view, Trim Castle, County Meath.

strategic obstacles if the castle was to be captured. Firstly, the curtain wall had to be breached. Secondly, the open bailey had to be safely crossed, and finally the keep itself had to be forced open and taken. Trim Castle in County Meath, offers an excellent example of a typical medieval castle layout. Here, all three elements are present. A powerful keep is positioned near the centre of a large triangular-shaped bailey. The bailey is enclosed by an extensive curtain wall, which incorporates a range of circular wall towers, as well as a pair of strong gatehouses (Fig. 1).

WALLING

One way to understand the structure and form of the Irish castle is to consider how it was built. This was achieved in a series of construction stages that included the walls, the floors and the roof, all of which incorporated defensive considerations. The first stage in the construction work was the building of the walls. These were built with heavy masonry that frequently exceeded 3 metres in thickness. As the walls were being built, a number of components were incorporated into the thickness. These included a batter, passageways, galleries, doors, window openings, and finally the roof-level battlements.

The batter was an outward slope at the base of the external walling. This added strength to the wall, but also had a defensive purpose. In times of attack, the defenders could drop missiles down from the top of the walls and these would be deflected outwards against attackers by the slope of the batter. Access from floor to floor and from room to room within the castle was provided by narrow passageways or stone stairways built into the walls. The staircases were often circular in layout and were commonly housed in individual towers (Fig. 2). The passageways were deliberately dark and narrow so that they could be easily defended, should an attacker gain entrance to the interior of the castle.

Fig. 2: Stairs, Knappogue Castle, County Clare.

DOORS

As work on the walling progressed, the door and window openings were formed. The door openings were usually given semi-circular or pointed arches, into which were later fitted the wooden doors. These were inserted into the stone openings and secured by heavy sliding cross pieces. The entrance door was always the most vulnerable point in the castle defences, as it could easily be burnt down, or broken through with the aid of a battering ram. Because of this, a number of features were introduced to protect them from these dangers. An artificial trench or moat could be excavated outside of the doorway and around the perimeter of the castle. This was often filled with water, or left dry wherever water was scarce. The moat offered two obstacles to attacking troops. It provided a physical barrier that had to be crossed and at the same time discouraged the attackers from trying to undermine the castle walls. Dublin Castle, for example, had a water-filled moat fed from the River Liffey, while the rock-cut moat at Ferns Castle, in County Wexford, was dry. Access across the moat was by means of a wooden drawbridge, which could be raised or lowered by means of pulleys.

In addition to the moat and drawbridge, a portcullis or heavy vertically sliding grid was positioned immediately in front of the main door of the castle. This, like the drawbridge, could be raised or lowered as required. The restored entrance to Roscrea Castle in County Tipperary illustrates how the drawbridge, portcullis and gate worked together (Fig. 3). In a number of castles, such as at Ferns, the entrance doorway was positioned at the first-floor level, a practice that made the use of a battering ram almost impossible. In such cases, access to the castle door was provided by a wooden ramp and platform, which could incorporate its own drawbridge over the castle moat.

Fig. 3: Entrance, Roscrea Castle, County Tipperary.

WINDOWS

The castle windows were small and limited in number, particularly in the case of lower floors, where narrow slots, or loops, were all that was provided. These loops were meant more for defence purposes than for the provision of light as they offered a secure opening through which a defending bowman could fire on attackers (Fig. 4). During the seventeenth century, musket loops came into use. These were small circular openings in the castle wall through which musket fire could be directed. In a number of instances, loops were set into an embrasure. That was a small alcove built into the thickness of the castle wall, that allowed a defender clear space in which to manoeuvre his bow or crossbow.

In addition to the loops, a machicolation was often incorporated into the walling. This was a small stone-built chamber that projected outwards from the main castle wall. The chamber was equipped with loops on all three sides as well as holes in the floor (Fig. 5). The fact that the chamber jutted out from the castle wall, offered the defenders the choice of outwards, downwards or flanking fire. This facilitated the protection of any weak points in the castle defences, such as wall corners or door openings. Where these projecting chambers were positioned in corner positions they are referred to as bartizans.

Where windows were provided, they were placed high up in the wall, or in sheltered positions for defensive reasons. The simplest and most common type of window consisted of a single opening with a flat or arched head (Fig. 6). Windows with double openings were also common, although they were frequently more decorative in design, such as in Bunratty Castle, County Clare, where two pointed arched openings are linked together (Fig. 7). A hood moulding was sometimes built over windows and external doorways. This was a projecting moulding placed directly over the window or door opening so as to deflect rainwater.

In the later castles of the sixteenth century, defence played a reduced role and large windows became common. Some of the windows in Leamaneh Castle in County Clare, for example, had no fewer than eight openings (Fig. 8). It is not clear how the castle windows were made weatherproof. The probability is that wooden shutters were used in inclement weather and animal skins in the dryer summer.

Fig. 4: Loop, Bunratty Castle, County Clare.

Fig. 5: Machicolation.

Fig. 6: Single opening window, Tower House, Ardee, County Louth.

Fig. 7: Double opening window, Bunratty Castle, County Clare.

Coolock Branch Tel: 8477781

Fig. 8: Multi-opening window, with hood, Leamaneh Castle, County Clare.

GARDEROBES

In addition to the passageways and galleries a number of castles had a garderobe built into the walls. This was a small privy, which was located at the end of a narrow passage. The privy itself consisted of a stone or wooden seat with a hole that drained through the castle wall and discharged onto the outside face of the structure. In terms of use, the garderobe was probably reserved for the exclusive use of the castle owner and his family.

FIREPLACES

Few of the early castles were provided with fireplaces and chimneys. Instead, a fire was placed in a metal cradle, or brazier, in the top storey. The brazier was placed on a large flat stone in the middle of the room, to reduce the risk of fire, and the smoke escaped through a hole in the roof. It was only during the fifteenth century that integral fireplaces and chimneys first made their appearances. In the case of older buildings, the fireplace and chimney were added, often in existing window openings, while in new buildings they were incorporated into the walling.

BATTLEMENTS

The final masonry components to be laid in place were the battlements, or crenellations. These were the parapets that crowned the castle walls at roof level, so as to offer a protective shield to the defenders in times of attack. The early Anglo-Norman crenellations consisted of shoulder-high parapets, behind which was constructed a wall walk. Later on, the parapet walls were pierced with a series of regular notches that allowed the defenders openings through which they could direct their fire against any attackers. These notched parapets also gave the castles one of their most characteristic and recognisable features: stepped crenellations (Fig. 9). The early notched crenellations, however, had one weakness. The defenders were exposed to enemy fire, particularly if they had to lean out over the wall to fire directly down.

Fig. 9: Simple crenellations.

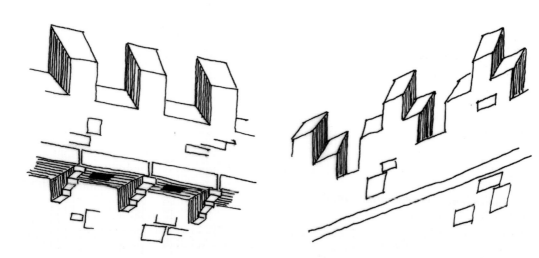

Fig. 10: Projected crenellations.

Fig. 11: Doubled-stepped crenellations.

In order to counteract this danger, a system of wooden platforms and hoardings was built around the crenellations. This was roofed over and extended out over the castle wall. The sides and the roof of the structure protected the defenders from attacking fire, in addition to which the floor had a series of holes that allowed missiles to be dropped directly down on the attackers.

Later, during the fourteenth century, the crenulations were modified and the wooden structures could be dispensed with. The parapet wall was moved forward of the main line of the wall and supported by means of projecting corbels, while at the same time openings were left in the floor (Fig. 10). These floor openings allowed the defenders to drop missiles down on an enemy, while they themselves were shielded behind the crenellations. The design of crenellations was further advanced during the fourteenth century, particularly in Ireland, when it became common to provide double-stepped parapets. This arrangement shielded the head, shoulders and body of the defenders (Fig. 11).

FLOORS

As the castle walling began to rise, the floors were inserted. These consisted mostly of wooden floorboards which were laid on heavy wooden joists. The joists were carried on wall plates, which were in turn supported by stone corbels that projected out from the walls (Fig. 12). Stone vaulting was occasionally used, although sparingly. This consisted of stone arches, or vaulting, that spanned the width of a floor. The vaulting offered a fireproof floor and also helped to strengthen the adjoining masonry walling.

Fig. 12: Wooden flooring from below, Cahir Castle, County Tipperary.

Fig. 13: Reconstructed roof, Cahir Castle, County Tipperary.

ROOFS

When the stone walling was complete, work started on the wooden roof. The roof at Dunsoughly Castle in County Dublin is one of the few in Ireland to have survived from the Middle Ages. It consists of a series of heavy wooden trusses that were spaced about 2 metres apart (Fig. 13). These trusses supported the rafters and these in turn were sheeted on the outside with wooden boarding. Finally the boarding was faced externally with slates, although wooden shingles and thatch were sometimes used. Once the roof was complete the castle was ready to receive the owner, his family and the garrison.

MURDER HOLE

One defence feature not mentioned so far, is the murder hole. This consists of a hole in a floor through which defenders could fire on attackers who have gained access to the level below. This is a common feature, particularly in the floor immediately over entrance chambers.

TIMESCALE

In looking at Irish medieval castles, it must be remembered that their construction took place in the period between the thirteenth and the seventeenth centuries. During this time most of the castle structures underwent extensions and changes. In fact, there is hardly a castle that has not experienced some degree of addition or modification. For example, freestanding great halls have been added to the initial layout at Adare and Askeaton Castles in County Limerick and extra storeys have been added to Trim Castle in County Meath and Athenry Castle in County Galway. In addition to these extensive changes, there are numerous examples of new windows and fireplaces being inserted. For this reason, the dating of some castles is not always obvious. For example the keep of Doe Castle in County Donegal was originally a sixteenth-century tower house to which the bailey, curtain wall and domestic accommodation were added in the following century.

ATTACK AND DEFENCE

In times of attack, the defending garrison were safe behind the protection of the walls and crenellations and could rely on their personal weapons to fight off any attackers that succeeded in scaling or penetrating the walls. These personal weapons included: swords, shields, lances, longbows, and crossbows. Likewise, the attackers relied on their personal weaponry, but needed the assistance of siege engines, if they were to successfully breach the castle walls. These engines could include: scaling ladders, a battering ram, a siege tower, a mangonel, and a trebuchet.

The battering ram could consist of a heavy beam slung with ropes between a wheeled wooden framework. The machine could be manoeuvred up to the castle wall, where the ropes allowed the ram to be swung backwards and forward so as to pound the gate or other weak point. In the more elaborate battering rams, the top and sides of the framework could be sheeted with wood to protect the attackers from the defending fire.

The siege tower was a tall moveable wooden structure designed to help the attackers storm a section of the castle wall. The tower was sheeted with protective boarding and had a series of internal ladders that provided access to a top storey, which contained a drawbridge. Ideally the tower was built so that the top storey was level with the castle wall. In an attack, the tower was wheeled directly up to the wall, the drawbridge was lowered, allowing the attackers access to the wall top.

The mangonel was a medieval artillery piece used to hurdle heavy rocks against the castle walls. The machine operated on a crossbow like mechanism and consisted of a long beam, or throwing arm; with a spoon-like container at one end. The arm was arranged vertically with a pivot at the bottom and was attached to the wings of the crossbow by cables. In order to fire, the beam was winched backwards to the horizontal position and locked. This put considerable tension on the crossbow wings. The missile was then placed in the container and the locking mechanism released, whereupon the arm was pulled upright with considerable force and the missile discharged.

The trebuchet acted like a slingshot and was powered by a falling weight. It also consisted of a throwing arm with the heavy weight at one end and a long slingshot at the other. The arm was balanced at mid-point like a see-saw and the heavy weight held the arm in an upright position. When the machine was being used, the weight was lifted until the slingshot end was in the lower position, at which point the slingshot could be loaded with a heavy stone or similar missile. The weight was released and this jerked the arm into the vertical position. This had the effect of launching the missile that had been placed in the slingshot. The advantage of the trebuchet was that it could discharge its missile high over the castle walls, whereas the mangonal could only propel its missile at a low level.

Mining was another technique used by forces attacking a castle. The miner's task was to dig a tunnel under the castle wall so as to undermine and destabilise it. The miners dug their tunnel until they reached a point directly beneath the castle walls. There they used wooden beams to support the overhead walling. They then set fire to the beams and retreated back through the tunnel to safety. Eventually, the fire burnt through the beams and this caused the overhead walls to collapse. The attacking troops could then focus their attention on the damaged part of the castle wall. In this context, it is worth noting that the corners of the castle building were particularly vulnerable to mining; and this was one of the reasons that influenced the building of circular, rather than square, corner and wall towers.

TWO

THE MOTTE-AND-BAILEY

1200–1300

THE ANGLO-NORMAN COLONY

In the late twelfth and early thirteenth centuries the Anglo-Normans fought their way across the Irish landscape and carved out a new colony for themselves. These invaders are historically referred to as Anglo-Normans because most of the leaders and supporters came from England and Wales, rather than directly from Normandy. The Anglo-Normans initially arrived in Ireland as mercenaries, to help the deposed Dermot McMurrough retake his Kingdom of Leinster. They secured the kingdom for Dermot, but afterwards decided to stay and extend their activities. In the 1170s Anglo-Norman forces had taken Cork, Limerick and East Ulster. Towards the middle of the next century both Kerry and Galway had also been secured, but it was not until about 1300 that Sligo and Donegal fell. By this period the expansion of the Anglo-Norman colony had reached its furthest extent, although even then, only about two-thirds of the country came under direct Anglo-Norman rule, while the rest remained under Gaelic control.

THE MOTTE-AND-BAILEY

When the Anglo-Normans conquered a fresh territory, they needed to establish a strategic and secure base as quickly as possible. To achieve this, they often built a temporary post or castle: a motte-and-bailey. This was a type of temporary defended structure, more like a fort than a castle, which had been developed earlier by the Normans in France and England. It consisted essentially of two earth-built mounds joined together, on which a number of wooden structures were built. The motte was the taller of the two mounds. It was circular in plan and had a flat top, the whole much like an upturned bowl in outline. The bailey, in contrast, was much lower. It was larger in area than the motte and was usually oval or rectangular in plan.

A wooden tower was erected on the crown of the motte and this was enclosed by a wooden palisade or stockade that extended around the flat edge of the mound. Lower down, the bailey acted as courtyard and, like the motte, it was also was enclosed by a wooden palisade. The different levels of the structure were connected by a wooden stairway and it was also protected by a palisade. In addition, a deep moat was excavated around the entire structure. The wooden tower on the motte provided living quarters for the commander, while the bailey provided accommodation and protection for the remainder of the garrison (Fig. 14).

The advantage of the motte-and-bailey was that it could be speedily erected, within a week or less. The necessary material, the clay for the mounds and the wood for the palisade and tower, could be drawn from the immediate landscape. In operational terms, the moat was probably dug first. The spoil from the excavation helped to provide clay for the mounds, although existing topographical features such as a natural mound, or a native-built ring fort, were frequently used

Fig. 14: Conjectural view, Motte-and-Bailey.

as a ready-made base. The entire building operation therefore required only a supply of labourers, supplemented by a few experienced woodworkers.

In a number of cases, such as Lorrah, County Tipperary and Callen, County Kilkenny, mottes without baileys were erected. The reasons for the absence of baileys in these cases are uncertain, but may have resulted from a rush to complete the structure quickly. Alternatively, the motte alone may have been considered sufficient to offer protection for a small holding garrison. This practice of building a motte without a bailey was particularly common in East Ulster. In contrast to this, a small number of structures, such as Donaghmoyne in County Monaghan included a second or outer bailey.

DISTRIBUTION AND SURVIVAL

The remains of about 300 motte-and-bailey sites survive around the Irish landscape. The highest density occurs in East Ulster and the Louth/Meath areas, with a thin scattering distributed elsewhere across the country. The scale of the motte-and-baileys varied with the resources of

Fig. 15: Motte-and-Bailey, Granard, County Longford.

Fig. 16: Motte at Nobber, County Meath.

the builders, with examples at Granard in County Longford (Fig. 15) and Knockgraffon in County Tipperary even today offering impressive structures.

In most cases the remains of isolated mounds are all that survive on the landscape. The wooden buildings and the palisades have of course long since decayed and the earthworks have very often slipped and partially filled in the moat. Also, many examples have suffered extensive damage or destruction through human activity. For example the bailey at Nobber in County Meath was partially removed to make way for housing and a library (Fig. 16), while the bailey at St Mullins in County Carlow has been badly damaged through quarrying.

One of the difficulties with the motte-and-bailey, in terms of defensive strategy, was that it offered only a limited degree of protection in times of attack. It could withstand an assault by a lightly equipped raiding party, but the garrison could quickly be overwhelmed in a concentrated effort. Particularly as the wooden structures were extremely vulnerable and could be set on fire. This was overcome in some instances such as at Shanid in County Limerick and Clonmacnoise in County Westmeath, when the wooden structures were later replaced with stonework. Elsewhere, as the Anglo-Norman presence was consolidated, the building of large and substantial stone-built castles on green-field sites became the common practice of both the Crown and the individual Anglo-Norman families.

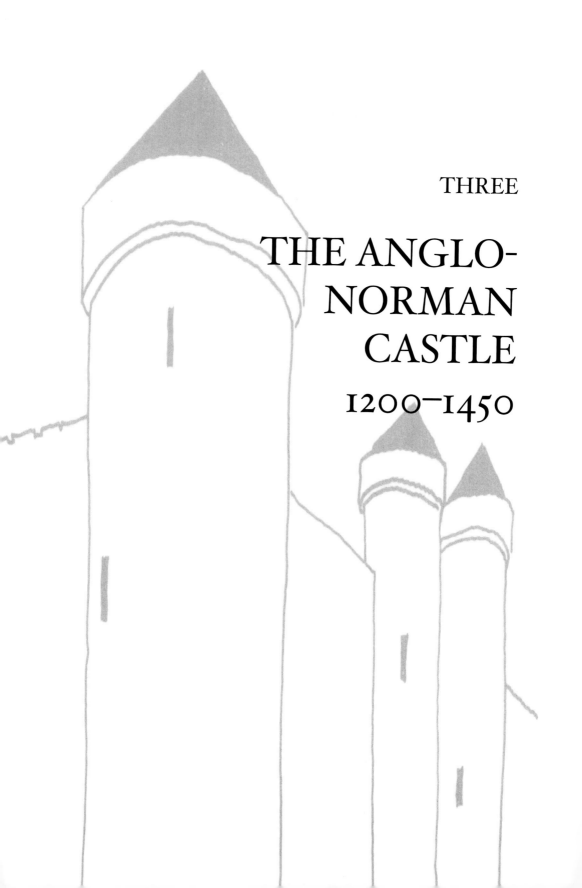

THREE

THE ANGLO-
NORMAN
CASTLE

1200–1450

STONE CASTLES

The Anglo-Normans had acquired considerable skills in stone-castle building during their earlier military experiences in England and Wales, and on the Crusades. Hense when the conquest of Ireland got underway, they brought these skills with them and applied them. Most of these early stone-built castles were built by the leading Anglo-Norman barons such as de Lacy, de Courcy and Marshall, while others were built on the orders of the Crown. The form of the stone castle more or less followed the earlier motte-and-bailey arrangement and for the most part included a keep set in a protective bailey. The stone castles were, however, much larger in scale than the motte-and-baileys and they fall into three distinct types: castles with a keep and bailey, castles with a bailey but no keep, and castles with a keep and no bailey.

CASTLES WITH KEEPS AND BAILEYS

The castle at Trim in County Meath is by far the largest of the Anglo-Norman castles in Ireland and consists essentially of three main elements. These include a massive keep, an extensive triangular-shaped bailey and an extensive curtain wall (Fig. 17). Hugh de Lacy began work on the structure in about 1190 and he chose an elevated site on the west bank of the River Boyne. Unfortunately the structure is now in a much-ruined condition. Despite this, it still projects a powerful image of Anglo-Norman strength and military power.

The massive keep was built on a mound outside of which a moat was excavated. The main block of the building is square in plan with square towers extending outwards from each side in a cross-like arrangement (Figs 18 & 19). Entrance to the keep is through the east tower, which originally had a fore building that has now disappeared. Internally, the keep was three storeys high. The ground and first floors were divided into two chambers by a cross wall, while the top floor consisted of a large single room. The projecting side towers contained smaller chambers, such as the chapel on the first floor of the entrance tower, and access to the various rooms and floors was by means of a complicated arrangement of stairs and wall passages. The keep had very few windows and most of the openings consisted of loops with splayed embrasures internally.

The bailey at Trim also contains the remains of some later ancillary buildings. One of these is the rectangular-arranged great hall, which was built abutting the north corner tower in about 1300. Today little survives of the hall except the wall stumps and the filled-in decorated windows on the east wall.

The great strength of Trim Castle lay in the extensive curtain wall. This has three rectangular towers along the eastern riverfront edge and six round towers along the remaining sides (Fig. 20). Outside the wall, the river on the east side acted as a natural barrier, while the line of the river was carried around the remaining sides in the form of a moat. The castle had two barbican-type gatehouses of which only the southern one survives. This consists of a square tower built on the outside of the moat with a second larger circular tower positioned on the line of the curtain wall.

A walled and roofed passage spans the moat and links the two towers together (Fig. 21). Access through the barbican was complex and is worth noting. The initial entrance door was positioned on the outer tower. This was placed at first-floor level and was reached from the ground by means of a sloped platform. Inside the door, a complex system of drawbridges, portcullises and doors allowed visitors to pass through the structure into the bailey, while the upper levels of the structure contained the mechanisms for the drawbridges and portcullises. Other excellent examples of castles built with central keeps like Trim include: Athenry in County Galway, Dunamase in County Laois and Glanworth in County Cork.

The castle at Athenry was built by Meiler de Birmingham in about 1238 and has recently been very successfully restored, with the exception of the ruined hall on the south side (Fig. 22). The keep was positioned in the centre of an approximately square bailey and built in a series of stages. The ground level was built in about 1235 and this was followed a few years later by a second storey. Later still, a third and attic story was added to the structure. The internal stairs are a reconstruction, but the stone stairs to the roof top still survives. Externally the squat-looking keep has a pronounced batter as well as a heavily decorated door and windows (Fig. 23). The entrance door is at first-floor level and this is accessed from the ground by recently erected wooden stairs.

Carrickfergus Castle in County Antrim, offers an example of a castle where, in contrast to Trim, the keep is incorporated into the line of the curtain wall. It is second only to Trim in scale and impressiveness, and it is positioned on a rocky promontory that juts into Belfast Lough (Fig. 24). The castle was started in the late twelfth century by John de Courcy and developed in a series of progressive stages that, over time, extended over the entire surface of the rock.

The formative late-twelfth-century structure consisted of the massive square keep with a small bailey positioned on the southern end of the rock. The keep was placed in the north-west corner of the bailey and remains the outstanding feature of the castle. It is square in plan and extends to four storeys high (Fig. 25). Internally the ground, first and second floors are divided into a pair of rectangular rooms, while the top floor consists of a large hall with the roof over (Fig. 26). Entrance to the keep is by means of external stairs to the first floor. The circular stairs in the south-west corner provides access to the other floors (Fig. 27). There is also a system of secondary stairs in the north-west angle which gives access to the garderobes on the second and top storeys. The windows of the upper floor are particularly interesting and consist of a pair of rounded arches framed within a larger overarch (Fig. 28). The great hall was built along the east curtain wall, but this was later demolished.

During the first half of the thirteenth century the castle was extended northwards in two stages. The second, or middle, bailey was added in the first phase. This was achieved by extending a new wall across the full width of the promontory. The new wall contained two towers, one in the centre and one at the eastern end. The third or outer bailey was created by extending the line of the earlier curtain wall northwards along the irregular outline of the rock, to terminate at a new gatehouse at the landward end (Fig. 29). This was given of a pair of double-storey circular towers with an arched passageway between as well as a drawbridge, a portcullis and a wooden gate. Today the castle is in an excellent state of preservation in terms of structure and atmosphere.

Other good examples of castles where the keep was built on the line of the curtain wall include: Cahir and Nenagh castles in County Tipperary, Carlingford and Castleroche Castles in County Louth, and Adare and Dungarvan Castles in counties Limerick and Waterford respectively.

Cahir Castle was built on a small island on the River Suir, probably by William of Worcester in the thirteenth century. Like Carrickfergus, the building was completed in a sequence of phases. The original structure consisted of a square bailey, with four corner towers as well as a gatehouse on the south curtain wall. Initially the east corner tower acted as the keep, but the gatehouse was converted into a much larger keep during the fifteenth century. At about the same time the lines of the curtain wall were extended southwards to take in a new middle and outer bailey (Fig. 30). The entire structure has been extensively restored and is in a very fine state of preservation. With its riverside position, expansive curtain wall, range of buildings, tall towers, and crenellations, it offers a dramatic portrait of a medieval castle (Fig. 31).

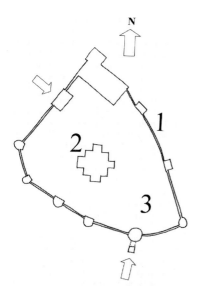

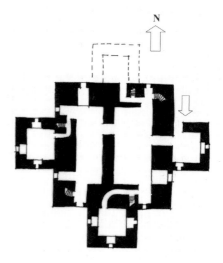

Fig. 18: Ground-floor plan, Trim Castle, County Meath.

Fig. 17: Plan, Trim Castle, County Meath.
(1: curtain wall, 2: keep, 3: bailey).

Fig. 19: The keep, Trim Castle, County Meath.

Fig. 20: Wall towers, Trim Castle, County Meath.

Fig. 21: Barbican, Trim Castle, County Meath.

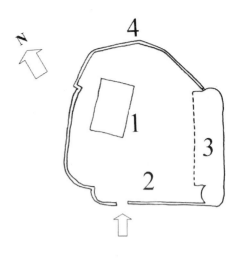

Fig. 22: Layout, Athenry Castle, County Galway.
(1: keep, 2: bailey, 3: hall, 4: curtain wall.)

Fig. 23: Keep, Athenry Castle, County Galway.

Fig. 24: Carrickfergus Castle, County Antrim.

Fig. 25: Keep, Carrickfergus Castle, County Antrim.

Fig. 26: Top floor, Carrickfergus Castle, County Antrim.

Fig. 27: Stairs, Carrickfergus Castle, County Antrim.

Fig. 28: Window, Carrickfergus Castle,
County Antrim.

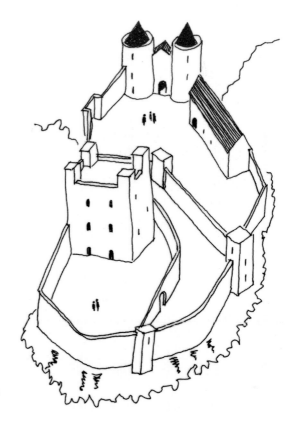

Fig. 29: Layout, Carrickfergus
Castle, County Antrim.

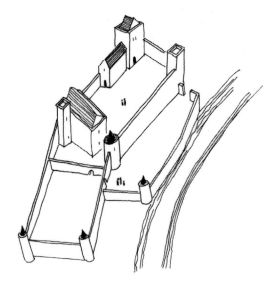

Fig. 30: Layout, Cahir Castle, County Tipperary.

Fig. 31: Cahir Castle, County Tipperary.

CASTLES WITH BAILEYS AND NO KEEPS

This second type of castle constructed during the Anglo-Norman period includes: Dublin, Kilkenny, Limerick, Roscrea, Roscommon, and Swords town castles, as well as Balintubber, County Roscommon and Ballymoon, County Carlow. All were built without keeps and the residential and administrative accommodation of the castle was incorporated into one or more of the curtain-wall towers.

King John's Castle in Limerick was built expressly for King John and work started in about 1200. The structure was positioned on the east bank of the River Shannon and was defended by a river-fed moat that extended around the landward sides. The layout consisted of an almost square bailey enclosed by a curtain wall, with a massive circular tower at each corner (Fig. 32). The castle entrance is on the north curtain wall and consists of a powerful twin-towered gatehouse with an arched gateway. In the early sixteenth century, the south-western corner tower was demolished and was replaced with a low arrow-shaped tower or bastion. Around the same time, the heights of the riverside towers were reduced. In the twentieth century, part of the east curtain wall was removed and this is now the site of the recently built museum. The castle has been successfully restored and despite the various changes it still presents a formidable approach from the County Clare side (Fig. 33).

The castle at Kilkenny in County Kilkenny was also built without a keep. Work was started by William Marshall in about 1207 on an elevated site that overlooked both the River Nore and Marshall's new town. The layout consisted of an approximately rectangular bailey, enclosed by a tall curtain wall and a moat. Like Limerick, there was a massive round tower at each corner and a twin-towered gateway on the south side (Fig. 34). Unfortunately, Marshall's original structure has suffered considerable alterations. The moat, the south-east towers, and the south-east curtain wall were removed to give the castle its current U-shaped plan. At the same time, a new classical gateway was inserted in the west wall and a range of new domestic buildings were constructed around the inside of the curtain wall. At the same time the towers and curtain wall were pierced with large windows and the walls were topped with new Romantic-style battlements. Despite these extensive amendments, Kilkenny Castle still manages to project a strong medieval presence in terms of scale, mass, form, and atmosphere.

The castle at Swords in County Dublin is another keep-less castle that has recently been successfully restored (Fig. 35). It was built by John Comyn, Archbishop of Dublin in about 1200

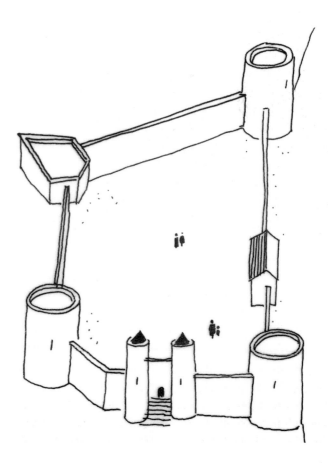

Fig. 32: Layout, King John's Castle, Limerick.

Fig. 33: King John's Castle, Limerick.

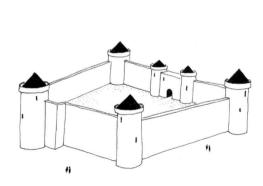

Fig. 34: Conjectural layout, Kilkenny Castle,
County Kilkenny.

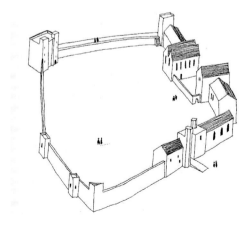

Fig. 35: Layout, Swords Castle, County Dublin.

Fig. 36: Warden's Tower, Swords
Castle, County Dublin.

Fig. 37: Conjectural view, Carlow Castle,
County Carlow.

Fig. 38: Carlow Castle, County Carlow.

and consists of an approximately square-shaped bailey, with a group of domestic and ecclesiastical buildings arranged along the south and east curtain walls (Fig. 36). These are very complex and consist of a gatehouse, small residential towers, a chapel, and great hall. There is also a double-story warden's tower on the north-western corner of the curtain wall (Fig. 37). Roscrea Castle in County Tipperary is similar in plan to Swords. It was built by the Crown in about 1280 and consists of an approximately rectangular bailey, enclosed by an irregular curtain wall that incorporates a restored gatehouse (Fig. 38) and two circular wall towers.

CASTLES WITH KEEPS AND NO BAILEYS

The third type of castle built by the Anglo-Normans includes those where only a keep was provided, without the protection of a bailey. Included in this group are the castles at Carlow Town, Ferns in County Wexford and Lea in County Laois, as well as the small Castle Kirk, Shrule and Coolhull Castle in Counties Mayo and Wexford respectively.

When Marshall began his castle at Carlow he based the plan on the layout of Kilkenny, but much reduced in terms of scale. The idea of the four circular corner towers was retained, but what was previously the courtyard was completely taken up by a solid residential block, or keep. In other words, the castle consisted of a single rectangular building with circular towers at each corner (Fig. 37). Like Kilkenny, Carlow Castle was positioned on a prominent rise and dominated both the adjoining River Barrow and Marshall's new town of Carlow. The entrance was positioned on the first floor and was probably accessed by a wooden ramp and platform. The castle seems to have had three floors and access between them was by means of a stone staircase. The structure measured approximately 17 metres by 10 metres internally and the arrangement probably had wooden floors and partitions, as well as a slated wooden roof.

Regretfully, only part of Carlow Castle survived an attempt to convert the structure into a mental hospital in the early nineteenth century. The proposal was poorly executed and half the castle was accidentally blown down with dynamite, leaving only the west wall and the two corner towers standing. Nevertheless, the ruin, when viewed from the street, offers a clear impression of the original structure. This includes the two corner towers, the massive stone wall, and parts of the battlements (Fig. 38).

The surviving structure of Ferns Castle is more substantial than at Carlow and includes the two southern corner towers, as well as parts of the south, east and north walls (Fig. 39). The keep was larger than that at Carlow and measured 20 metres by 18 metres internally. As is the case with Carlow, the building had three floors, with the entrance at the first floor. Again similar to Carlow, access between the floors was by means of a staircase incorporated into the tower walls. Three surviving elements of Ferns Castle are of particular interest. The south-east tower contains a superbly vaulted chapel with decorated ribs and traceried windows and the surviving walls offer a range of decorated pointed windows and cross loops (Fig. 40). In addition, the dramatic rock-cut moat still stretches along a section of the south wall. Unfortunately the castle is now in a very ruined condition and only part of the shell survives. Despite this, the two towers and parts of the walling offer a dramatic impression of the original structure.

Lea Castle is smaller than the two previous examples, but is the only one of the Marshall castles where the complete outline of the keep can be seen. Unfortunately, only one corner of the structure survives to anywhere near its full height. The internal dimensions of the keep measure approximately 14 metres by 10 metres. The ground floor is divided into two equal-sized chambers by a central masonry partition, although nothing survives of the remainder of the

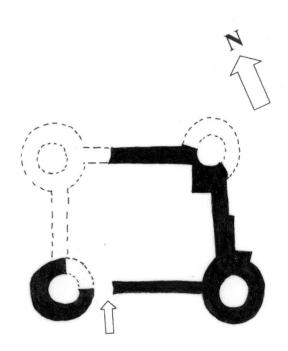

Fig. 39: Outline plan, Ferns Castle,
County Wexford.

internal structure, which was in all probability wooden.

Castle Kirk in County Mayo and Coolhull in County Wexford are two of a number of small castles that do not contain a bailey and to which the term 'Hall House' has been given. Castle Kirk was probably built during the thirteenth century and is now a ruin (Fig. 41). The structure was originally two storeys high with a single room on each floor. The entrance door was at first-floor level and it was reached by a stone staircase. The internal access between the upper and lower levels is by means of circular stairs in the north-west corner. There is a garderobe on the ground and first floor and the first floor is lit by a system of narrow windows with embrasures. A curious feature is the square buttresses at each corner. These seem to serve no purpose except for the one on the north-west corner which holds the stairs. The ruined Coolhull Castle is similar in plan to Castle Kirk except that it is three storeys high and has an attached service tower. The service tower has an extra storey and contains circular stairs. In addition, the castle has extensive double-stepped crenellations (Fig. 42) and an impressive fireplace on the first-floor level.

The question of why castles like Ferns and Castle Kirk lacked a bailey is puzzling. There is no evidence of curtain walling ever having been provided in either example. However, it may very well be that a bailey was initially provided, but the enclosing wall may have been quarried in the past. Alternatively the curtain walls may have been wooden, in which case all traces have vanished. By the middle of the fourteenth century the medieval castle-building movement in Ireland paused. This was caused partially by the Black Death, the resurgence of Gaelic influence and the decline of the colony. Later on in the early fifteenth century, when castle building in Ireland resumed, a new and smaller type of castle appeared: the Tower House.

Fig. 40: Ferns Castle, County Wexford.

Fig. 41: First-floor plan, Castle Kirk, County Mayo.

Fig. 42: Coolhull Castle, County Wexford.

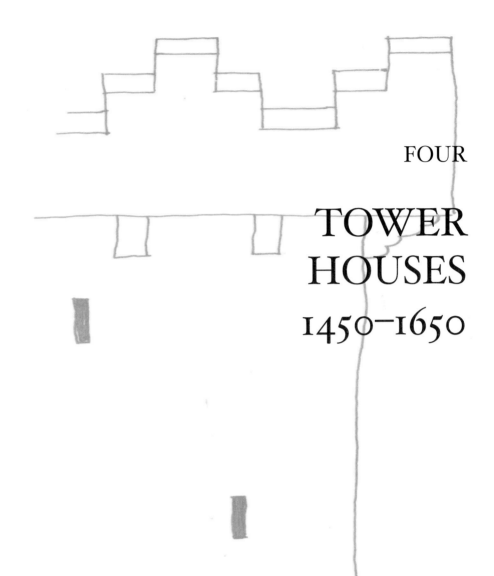

FOUR

TOWER
HOUSES
1450–1650

Coolock Branch Tel: 8477781

THE TOWER HOUSE

By the early years of the fifteenth century the Anglo-Norman (and subsequent English) colony had effectively shrunk to an area around Dublin called the Pale. In an attempt to hold onto this territory the English Crown offered a subsidy of ten pounds to any person who built a small castle or tower in the counties of Dublin, Meath, Kildare, and Louth. Initially the dimensions of the castle were to be 6 metres long, 5 metres wide and 12 or more metres in height, although these dimensions were later reduced. Whether the subsidy was ever paid is uncertain, but the initiative prompted the building of an extensive number of small castles, or tower houses. This tower house building movement was initially confined to the Pale, but the idea quickly spread across the country. In contrast to the earlier centuries, the tower houses were built by the smaller landowners of the period – both colonial and Gaelic alike. These builders lacked the resources of the earlier Anglo-Norman magnates and the modest scale of the tower houses reflected this difference. By and large, the tower houses can be seen as the castles of the minor landowning families.

The typical tower house consists essentially of a slim tower-like structure approximately 6 metres square in plan and four to six storeys in height (Fig. 43). This was very often enclosed by a small courtyard or bailey, in the case of the tower house often referred to as a bawn.

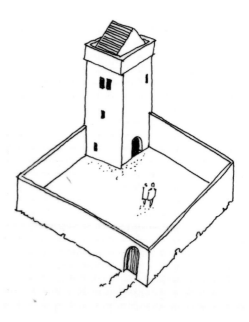

Fig. 43: Diagrammatic layout, typical Tower House.

The earlier tower houses, such as Clara and Aughnanure, conformed to a basic rectangular plan, although later examples, such as Roodstown, Blarney and Bunratty, expanded on this basic plan and incorporated increased floor areas as well as elaborate corner towers.

The internal layout of the tower house was elementary and consisted of a series of single rooms built one above the other. In many cases, access between the floors was by means of circular stone stairs that were built into the walls. In other cases, one or two corner towers were added. These often contained the stairs, small chambers and garderobes. Because of the modest scale of the tower house, the accommodation was limited. The ground floor was used for storage and the top storey acted as the hall. Elsewhere, the remaining floors were used mainly for domestic purposes. Apart from scale, the tower houses contained all of the earlier Anglo-Norman military-type features. These included: heavy masonry walling, a batter, arched doors, loops, narrow windows, embrasures, machicolations, crenellations, wall walks, and steeply pitched roofs. Defence was still a major consideration. In terms of numbers, tower houses make up the greatest number of Irish castles, with surviving examples running into the thousands. Of these, Ashtown, Clara, Aughnure, Rodstown, Bunratty, Ballymahon, and Blarney all offer examples that are particularly characteristic.

ASHTOWN

The recently restored fifteenth-century Ashtown Tower in the Phoenix Park in Dublin is a good example of a small basic tower house. It is three storeys high and consists of a single room on each floor with a small projecting tower at one corner (Fig. 44). The rooms are small and measure approximately 7 metres by 5 metres. Curiously, the building seems to have lacked a garderobe. The pointed entrance door is at ground level and this provides direct access into the ground-floor room. Opening off this, the corner tower provides access to the overhead rooms.

Fig. 44: Ashtown Tower House, Phoenix Park, Dublin.

The flooring and roof timbers throughout are restorations and present a clear illustration of how the original carpentry appeared. Light was provided to the interior of the towers by a small range of narrow windows and loops. The tower lacks stepped crenellations. Instead, a plain parapet shields the roof-level wall walk behind.

CLARA

Clara Castle in County Kilkenny is a little more complex. It stands five storeys high and is rectangular in plan. The ground, first, second, and third floors have a large main room with a smaller chamber attached, while the top floor is made up of a large single room – an internal arrangement typical of a great many tower houses (Fig. 45).

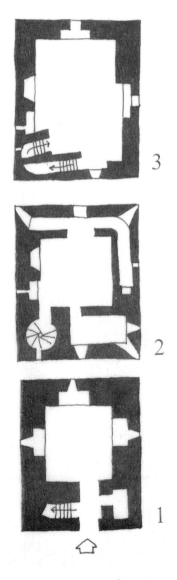

Fig. 45: Layout, Clara Tower House, County Kilkenny.
(1: ground floor, 2: second floor, 3: top floor.)

Fig. 46: Clara Tower House, County Kilkenny.

The pointed arched ground-level entrance door leads into a small lobby. Directly ahead is the main room, while on the right side is a small guard room. A stone circular staircase opens off the left side of the lobby and this rises to the top floor, servicing the other floors as it does. On the top floor the final stairs to the roof walk are reduced to a straight narrow flight. The tower has a garderobe on the second and third floor, each incorporated into the thickness of the wall. In addition, the third floor has a secret chamber, accessible only from the overhead floor. The floor of the top storey consists of a stone vault that spans the shortest width of the tower, while some of the remaining wooden floors still survive. A wooden roof originally extended between a pair of gabled end walls. The gables still survive, although the roof timbers no longer exist. The second and top floors both contain a fireplace, but these seem to be later additions.

From the outside it can be seen that the floors are lit by a mixture of loops and narrow round-headed windows (Fig. 46). The widest windows are on the upper floors while the ground-floor is served only by loops. Most of the windows and loops were provided with wide embrasures. The crenellations are double stepped and a roof-level machicolation protects the ground floor entrance doorway directly below. The base of the tower has a pronounced batter and a small bawn offers protection to the entrance side of the castle.

AUGHNANURE

Aughnanure in County Galway is similar in scale and plan to Clara. The defences are, however, much more elaborate, and the structure has been restored. The tower was built by the O'Flaherty family in around 1500 and it is six storeys high, with an internal arrangement similar to Clara. The ground floor has a single room, entrance lobby, guard room, and circular stone stairs rising from a corner position. Overhead the remaining floors have a single room with a small attached chamber. Four of the floors are served with a garderobe and the top floor consists of a single room.

The interior of the tower is lit by a range of small windows and loops. What is curious is that the entrance door, windows and loops on the north side are all symmetrically arranged, with equally sized openings placed directly one above the other at each level (Fig. 47). This is in contrast to the more common irregular arrangements of tower house window patterns. Another unusual feature is the four roof-level machicolations. Each of these is located at midpoint along the length of the four walls. The tower defences are also augmented by a pair of third-floor bartizans, one at each corner of the east wall.

Again in contrast to Clara, the Aughnanure Tower is enclosed by a large inner and outer bawn. This largely consists of an elaborate system of curtain walling and corner wall towers (Fig. 48). The River Drimneen acted as a natural moat along the north-west and south-west sides of the curtain wall, although one section of this has now dried up. The inner bailey encloses the tower and is wedge shaped. The curtain wall follows a zigzag course around the irregular riverside boundary, where part of the gatehouse survives. The walls on the opposite sides of the bailey

Fig. 47: Aughnanure Tower House, County Galway.

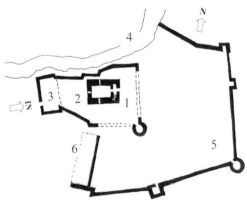

Fig. 48: Site Layout, Aughnanure Tower House, County Galway.
(1: tower house, 2: inner bailey, 3: gatehouse, 4: River Drimneen, 5: outer bailey, 6: ruin of hall.)

followed a more regular line with a single round tower at the south-east angle. Although the curtain wall at this point no longer exists, the corner tower with its pointed stone roof survives. The 'L-shaped' outer bailey wraps around the south-east corner of the inner bailey. The curtain wall here is more regular and incorporates four wall towers. A great hall once stood at the south-west corner, but apart from the east wall, it no longer exists.

ROODSTOWN

Roodstown Castle in County Louth differs from Clara and Aughnanure in that it incorporates two full-height corner towers. The plan is almost square and the internal layout follows the typical Clara and Aughnanure arrangements. The floor construction also differs from Clara in that the first floor is vaulted, while the remaining floors were wooden. The pointed arched entrance doorway is at ground-floor level and leads to a lobby from which access is provided to the single room and the stone stairs.

The outstanding feature of the castle is the two corner towers, which are positioned on diagonal corners of the main block and project above the wall-walk level (Fig. 49). One contains the garderobe, while the other houses the circular stairs that provide access to the various floors and the roof battlements. A curious aspect of the diagonal placing of the towers is that they fail to offer any form of flanking protection to the entrance. Externally, the tower lacks a batter (Fig. 50). The corner towers are lit by loops, while the rooms are provided with a range of small decorated arched windows. Unfortunately, the crenellations are much damaged.

Fig. 49: Roodstown Tower House, County Louth.

Fig. 50: First-floor plan, Roodstown Tower House, County Louth.

BUNRATTY

Bunratty Castle in County Clare is one of a group of particularly large and complex tower houses that incorporate a large main block as well as large towers at each of the four corners (Fig. 51). Others include Dunsoghly in County Dublin and Castletown in County Louth. The McNamara family started work on Bunratty in about 1467 and it was later taken over by the O'Briens. The tower stands on the banks of the River Bunratty and has been splendidly restored.

The central block contains a large room on each of the four floors. The ground floor held the castle stores and it was vaulted over, as is each of the three floors overhead. The castle is entered at the first-floor level by means of a raised reconstructed wooden platform and drawbridge. This floor and the floor above held a large hall, while above these the owner's apartment filled the top floor. The internal arrangements of corner towers are very complex. Each tower contains five floors and these are set at different levels to the main floor. Each one has a range of small chambers and a garderobe. In addition, each tower has adjoining circular stairs. These are built into the walls of the main block and serve both the main rooms and the towers (Fig. 52).

Externally, the castle lacks a pronounced batter and has a large range of mainly narrow windows and loops. The outstanding external feature is the wide and dramatic arches that stretch between the corner towers, high up, on the north and south sides. Another feature is the large windows immediately above the line of the arch. The roof and the double-stepped battlements are recent reconstructions.

BALLYNAHOW

Although most tower houses feature square or rectangular layouts, a small number were built with circular plans; these include Ballynahow in County Tipperary, Newtown in County Clare, and Balief in County Kilkenny.

Ballynahow seems to have been built by the Purcell family at some period in the sixteenth century. It is five storeys high with vaulting on two levels. A pointed arched doorway provides access into a lobby at ground level. This is built into the massive wall and leads to the single

Fig. 51: Bunratty Tower House, County Clare.

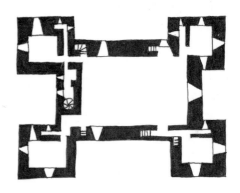

Fig. 52: First-floor plan, Bunratty Tower House, County Clare.

circular room on the same floor. The lobby also leads to the stairs which are built into the curve of the wall and serve the floors above. This staircase survives intact and allows the visitor to climb to the roof level. The upper floors are roughly rectangular in layout. The first floor has a fireplace and a small chamber built into the wall (Fig. 53). Externally the two lower floors are lit by little more than loops, while the upper levels have a number of small double- and single-pane windows (Fig. 54). The battlements have to a large extent perished and the roof was probably conical in shape.

BLARNEY

One of the difficulties with some tower houses is that they are not easily recognisable as such, as they may have been extensively altered or extended. The ruined Blarney Castle in County Cork, for example, is one of the better known Irish tower houses (Fig. 55). It is also one of the most complex as it was built in two separate phases. The building is L-shaped in plan and the initial phase consisted of a small tower, about 4 metres square internally, built on a high rocky site, in around 1480. Some time later, in about 1498, the second phase of the development was completed, when a much larger extension to was built on to the east side of Phase One, giving the overall structure its L-shaped plan (Fig. 56).

The internal layout of Phase One of the castle consisted of a single room, while the extension had a large hall with a small chamber at the northern end. The layout of the combined structure is, however, made twice as complicated by the fact that the two sections operated independently. Both have their own passages and staircases and the only internal link is by means of a single passage between the third floor of the original tower and the fourth floor of the extension. Later still, the structure was further amended by the insertion of a range of elaborate fireplaces and windows. The overall result is a confusing honeycomb of passageways, stairs, rooms and floor levels.

The floors throughout were a mixture of wood and stone vaulting, some of which have been removed. The windows are generally small double-paned openings, except for the projecting bay window on the north side of the original tower. Apart from the scale, the double-stepped crenellations are the most prominent feature of the castle. These are built on pointed corbels and extend well beyond the face of the main structure (Fig. 57). Parts of the original bawn survive, but this was modified by later work that included a now-burnt manor house as well as a circular tower.

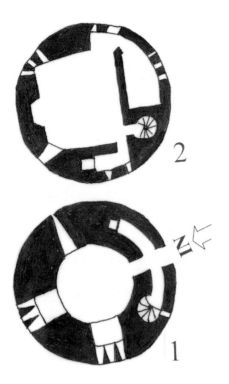

Fig. 53: Layout, Ballynahow Tower
House, County Tipperary.
(1: ground–floor plan, 2: first–floor
plan.)

Fig. 54: Ballynahow Tower House, County
Tipperary.

Fig. 55: Blarney Castle, County Cork.

Fig. 56: Second-floor plan, Blarney Castle, County
Cork.

Fig. 57: Crenellations, Blarney Castle, County Cork.

ARTILLERY

The introduction of gunpowder and artillery – particularly after 1600 – effectively brought castle building in Ireland to a close, as even the stoutest of castle walls could not withstand a sustained artillery barrage. The castle as a place of strategy and defence became obsolete and after 1650 only a few new castles were contemplated. This is not to say that defence considerations disappeared from Irish domestic building. On the contrary, the unstable 1600s saw the emergence of two further Irish castle forms: the Plantation castle and fortified house.

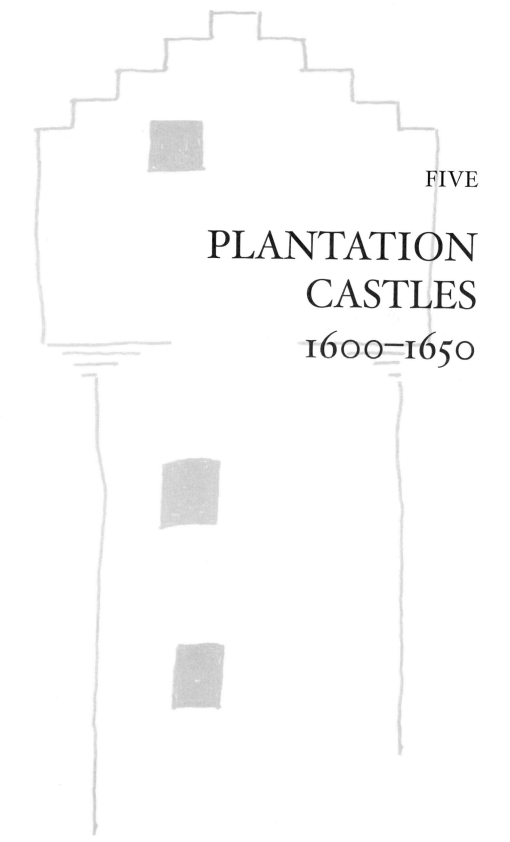

FIVE

PLANTATION
CASTLES
1600–1650

THE PLANTATION

During the seventeenth century the English Crown initiated a fresh and intense programme of colonisation of Ireland, so as to re-establish its control over the island. As part of this programme, the authorities introduced large numbers of English and Scottish settlers and planted them mainly in the northern counties. At the same time, the native Irish were driven from their lands to make way for the new arrivals. For this reason the period is referred to in Irish history as the 'Plantation'. The leaders of the new colonists, called 'undertakers', were given extensive land grants on condition that they secured their grants by erecting a castle or a fortified house, as well as a defended bawn. These Plantation castles were similar in scale to the tower houses, but differed in detail. They usually had a low tower set at one end of a small defended bawn, but the distinguishing features of the buildings included notable Scottish-like features. These often included T-shaped plans, steep crow-stepped gables, as well as pronounced circular and angle turrets. Brackfield in County Derry, Monea, Tully and Castle Balfour in County Fermanagh, Roughan in County Tyrone, Castle Baldwin in County Sligo, and Park's Castle in County Leitrim all offer typical examples of these Plantation castles.

BRACKFIELD CASTLE

The simple structure at Brackfield, immediately south of Derry, was built by Sir Edward Doddington and consisted of a plain small double-storey house set at one end of the bawn

Fig. 58: Conjectural view,
Brackfield Castle, County Derry.

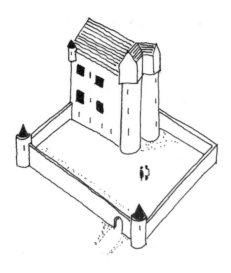

Fig. 60: Monea Castle, County Fermanagh.

Fig. 59: Conjectural view, Monea Castle, County Fermanagh.

(Fig. 58). The little block, now ruined, had a single circular corner tower at one end and a matching one on the diagonal corner of the enclosure.

MONEA CASTLE

The now-ruined castle at Monea was built by Revd Malcolm Hamilton in about 1618 and consists of a strong rectangular, four-storey block tucked into the corner of the bawn (Fig. 59). The ground floor held the kitchens and stores, above which the vaulted floor provided the living accommodation. The bedrooms were on the second floor, with extra rooms in the attic overhead.

The castle has a small circular turret placed high up on the east corner of the block, but the outstanding feature of the structure is the pair of tall cylindrical towers that were incorporated into the opposite west end. The towers are most unusual in that the top floor is square in shape and sits on corbelled courses that rise in steps from the circular part of the towers beneath (Fig. 60). Overhead, the square tops were crowned with crow-stepped gables. The entrance door is located in the north tower which also contains circular stairs. The little block also had two other staircases built into the side walling. Little remains of the windows, but these were narrow loops at ground level with simple rectangular openings higher up. The structure is now unroofed and only the base of the bawn wall survives, together with the outline of two corner towers.

TULLY CASTLE

Tully Castle in the same county was built by Sir John Hume in around 1612 and is similarly in ruins (Fig. 61). The block here is three storeys high including an attic and follows a T-shaped plan that sits in the northern end of the bawn (Fig. 62). The internal arrangement was similar to Monea, with the stores and kitchens at ground level, the residential accommodation on the first-floor level and the bedrooms in the overhead floors. The entrance and wooden stairs were located in the stem of the 'T'. Like Monea, the window openings are small and consist of loops at ground level as well as a mixture of single- and double-pane examples on the upper floors.

Fig. 61: Tully Castle, County Fermanagh.

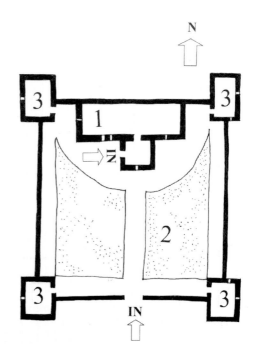

Fig. 62: Plan, Tully Castle, County
Fermanagh.
(1: castle block, 2: bawn, 3:corner
towers.)

In addition, steep gables define the roof lines. The walls of the bawn are mainly in ruins although the lower walls of the four rectangular corner towers survive. A formal geometric hedge garden has been recreated inside the bawn and this offers an impression of what the original garden probably looked like.

PARK'S CASTLE

In terms of scale, Park's Castle offers the most notable example of the Plantation-type castle. It dates from the early seventeenth century, is located near the edge of Lough Gill and has been successfully restored. The bawn is irregular in plan and the castle is positioned against one of the sides. The castle is rectangular in layout, with a square tower at one end and a circular tower at the other. The structure is three storeys in height except for the rectangular tower which extends an extra floor. The tower also provides the arched entrance to the castle and bawn (Fig. 63). The stores and kitchens are located at ground level, with the living and bedroom accommodation in the upper floors.

Externally small square loops provide light to the ground level, while the upper floors have a range of single- and double-paned windows. The main block of the castle has a simple pitched roof. The square tower has steep gables on all four sides, and the circular tower has a conical roof. The bawn walls are complete and have a single circular corner tower.

By the middle of the seventeenth century the short period of Plantation castle development was brought to a close by the Cromwellian and Williamite Wars. This was also the case outside of the northern counties where, during the early seventeenth century, a different form of castle building emerged: the fortified house.

Fig. 63: Diagrammatic layout, Park's Castle, County Leitrim.

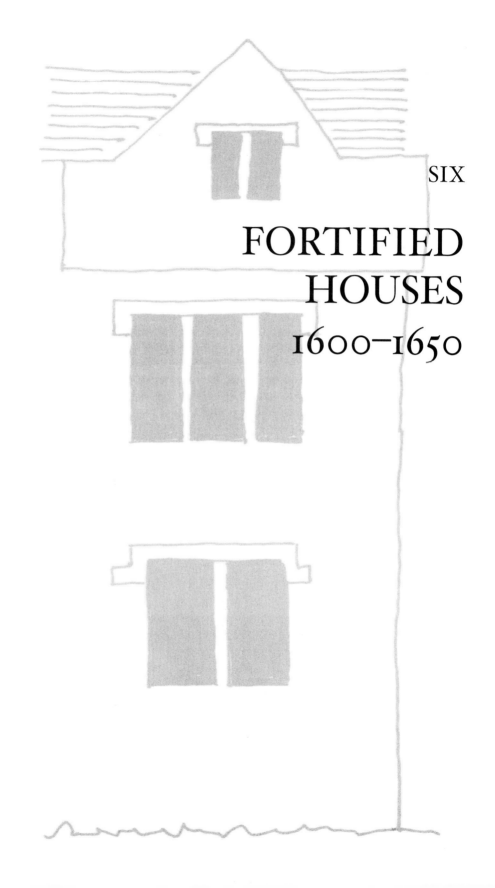

SIX

FORTIFIED
HOUSES
1600–1650

THE FORTIFIED HOUSE

Outside of the northern counties military conflict had virtually ceased as the first half of the seventeenth century progressed and defence considerations slowly gave way to comfort in castle building. Despite this, security remained a background influence and a new type of castle building appeared: the fortified house – part castle, part domestic house. This type of castle, like the earlier tower houses, was built by both English colonists and the native Gaelic chieftains.

The fortified houses differed from the earlier tower houses in that they included Tudor and Jacobean features, such as spacious and comfortable accommodation, as well as external string courses, and pronounced roof gables. More light was required and wide windows with hood mouldings were installed. These were frequently divided into panes by mullions and transoms. The former were slim stone uprights that divided the windows vertically. The latter were similar, but divided the windows horizontally. Fireplaces were now a standard feature with elaborate fire surrounds and tall diamond-shaped chimney stacks. All these new elements were imported from England and appeared in Ireland for the first time, although thick stone walling remained popular in line with the earlier medieval tradition.

The elevations of the fortified houses also incorporated the first movements towards the soon-to-follow Renaissance ideals. These included long block arrangements, as well as windows spaced equally apart and arranged directly one above the other. The main entrance doorway was framed with Renaissance decorations and its importance was emphasised by being positioned in the centre of the block. Notwithstanding these new influences, security was never completely abandoned as loops, bartizans, flanking projections and roof parapets were frequently, if discreetly, incorporated.

Irish fortified houses can be classified into two main categories. Firstly, earlier castles and tower houses where fortified house-type extensions were grafted on, such as Leamaneh and Donegal Castle; and secondly completely new buildings on green-field sites such as Carrick-on-Suir, Mallow, Burncourt, Coppingers Court, Kanturk, Portumna, and Rathfarnham. Unfortunately, as is often the case with earlier castles, all but a few of the fortified houses are in ruins.

CARRICK–ON–SUIR

Carrick-on-Suir, in County Tipperary is one of the earliest and by far the most domestic looking of the fortified houses. Initially the site consisted of a fifteenth-century castle, built near the north bank of the River Suir. This had an irregular-shaped bailey and a pair of towers on each corner of the north side. In about 1568 the Duke of Ormond extended the original castle by building a lavish fortified house onto this north side. The new structure was U-shaped in plan and butted against two older towers so as to incorporate an enclosed courtyard between the two (Fig. 64). The new building is two storeys high with an attic storey in the roof and measures about 30 metres across the front (Fig. 65). The house has been very successfully restored and offers an excellent example of its type, although the original castle is now in ruins.

The front elevation is symmetrically arranged with a projecting central bay, which contains the round-headed doorway at ground level. The line of the bay extends upwards to the first floor where it forms an extended bay window. Above this, the roof of the bay acts as a small balcony to the attic storey. The elevation on each side of the projecting bay has large mullion-type windows on each of the floor levels. The ground-level windows are divided into two panes, while the ones above are divided into three. Each pane has a curved head and the overall window openings have projecting hood mouldings.

The attic level has a rendered parapet with three high gables. Each of these is fitted with a central window like those at ground level, as well as a decorative stone finial at the crown of each gable. The sides of the building are similar in appearance to the front, with three gables, although they lack the symmetry. The western elevation has a central bay much like the entrance, but the bay on the opposite eastern side of the building is located to one side (Fig. 66).

Internally, the structure is only one room deep and the accommodation is arranged in large rooms spaced around the central courtyard. Many of these have decorated ceilings and plasterwork, as well as elaborate fireplaces. Access between the floors is provided by the staircase in the projecting bay on the west side, although communication between the ground floor rooms is not always direct. Despite the domestic scale and arrangement of the house, defence remained a consideration. This can be noted in the small round musket loops on the north front and the cross loops on the eastern bay (Fig. 67).

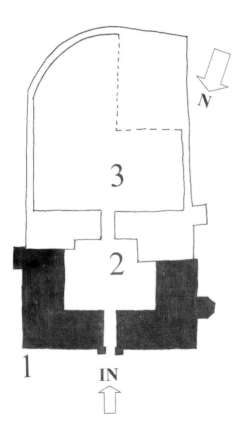

Fig. 64: Carrick-on-Suir Castle, County Tipperary.

Fig. 65: North elevation, Carrick-on-Suir Castle, County Tipperary.

Fig. 66: East elevation, Carrick-on Suir-Castle, County Tipperary.

Fig. 67: Musket loop, Carrick-on-Suir Castle, County Tipperary.

Fig. 68: Conjectural restoration, Leamaneh Castle, County Clare.

Fig. 69: Leamaneh Castle, County Clare.

LEAMANEH

Leamaneh Castle in County Clare consists of a fifteenth-century tower house, to which an oblong extension was added by Conor O'Brien in 1643 (Fig. 68). The original tower is rectangular in plan, five storeys high and has a pronounced batter. The interior was lit by a range of loops and small windows, with the round-headed doorway on the east side. The crenulations are ruined, but there is evidence of a roof level machicolation on the south side.

The elongated extension is four storeys high and was attached to the west side of the original tower (Fig. 69). The main southern elevation is irregular and features a range of windows. The round-headed doorway is positioned centrally on the combined structures, with two windows on the left and a single window on the right. Above this, a level of symmetry was achieved by positioning the first- and second-floor windows directly above the ground-floor windows and the door. There is a single string course between the second and the top floor and above this the attic story is defined by three large gables, with a window set in the centre of each. The windows are horizontally proportioned and capped by a hood moulding. Beneath the moulding, the windows are divided into individual panes by stone transoms and mullions. In addition to the windows and gables, the other interesting feature of note is the single bartizan on the third-floor level.

The castle had an extensive bawn, but this is now barely distinguishable, although the elaborate gate, which has a date stone of 1640, was demolished and re-erected in the grounds of nearby Dromoland Castle.

DONEGAL

Donegal Castle in Donegal town was similar in development to Leamaneh, although much more extensive in scale. The original tower house dates from around the fifteenth century and was built by member of the O'Donnell family on the banks of the River Eske. The tower was taken over by Sir Basil Brooke in 1616 and he developed his new home in two stages. First he remodelled the existing tower, which stood in the north corner of the bawn, and in about 1623 he added an extensive wing to one side of the tower (Fig. 70).

The O'Donnell tower followed the standard fifteenth-century internal arrangement, with a single large room on each floor. Brooke retained the basic rectangular outline of the tower, but made a number of significant changes. The entrance door on the east side was removed and a projecting bay was built in its place. This provided the base for a large bay window, which was inserted at the third-floor level. The original loops were retained on the first and second storeys, but the three levels above this were provided with wide transom and mullion windows.

The roof was extensively remodelled. A complex attic storey was added with three gables to the north-east and north-west elevation and a single gable on each of the remaining sides. In addition, a large, dramatically projecting bartizan was corbelled out from each of the four corners of the building.

The new extension was more complex and irregular than at Leamaneh. The extension itself is T-shaped with the top stroke of the T forming a projecting bay that butts against the south-west wall of the original tower. In effect this bay projects forward beyond the main line of the extension at the front and back (Fig. 71). It is probable that this small bay was built before the main extension.

Externally the elevation of the extension has three doorways to the front. One is round headed and positioned at the front of the projecting bay at ground-floor level. The second has a pointed arch. It is also at ground level, but near the far end of the block. The third doorway is round headed and decorated. It is on the first-floor level in an off-centre position. Presumably there was a wooden ramp or steps that provided access from the ground to the first-floor level. The windows throughout differ in size and spacing except for the single window in each of the five dramatic gables. All of these are divided into panes by a mixture of mullions and transoms.

Like Leamaneh, the internal planning is uncertain, as the original wooden floors and partitions no longer exist. However, there is a remarkable fireplace on the first floor of the original tower house with elaborately carved fruit and the coat of arms of Brooke and Leicester. The original tower house had an approximately rectangular bawn. Brooke seems to have strengthened this by following the course of the original wall. He also built a new gatehouse in the south corner, but retained the original tower in the opposite corner.

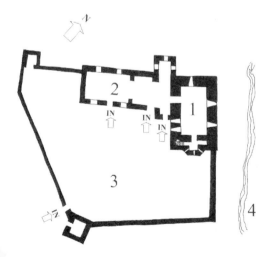

Fig. 70: Ground-floor plan, Donegal Castle, County Donegal.
(1: tower house, 2: extension, 3: bawn, 4: River Eske.)

Fig. 71: Conjectural restoration, Donegal Castle.

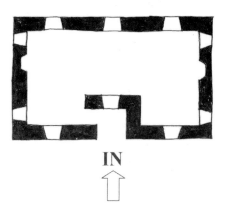

IN

↑

Fig. 73: Glinsk Castle, County Galway.

Fig. 72: Ground-floor plan, Glinsk Castle, County Galway.

GLINSK

Glinsk in County Galway is perhaps one of the earliest fortified houses in Ireland and offers a transitional link between the earlier tower houses and the fully developed fortified houses. The castle was built by the Burke family in about 1618 and has a curious layout. The plan consists of a basic rectangle about 20 metres by 10 metres, much like that of a tower house. However a shallow cut was incorporated into the centre of the south elevation and gave the block a U-shaped plan (Fig. 72). This also created the impression that this elevation consisted of a pair of corner towers.

The building had a basement, three upper floors and an attic storey in the roof. The internal arrangement is unknown as the wooden partitions and floors no longer exist. The attic had a pair of gables that spanned from the front to the rear of the building. These line up with the projecting sections of the south wall and emphasise the tower-like impression (Fig. 73). The remains of two roof-level bartizans can still be seen projecting from the southern corners, as well as a single corbelled machicolation in the centre of the north wall.

The basement of the house is lit by small loop-like openings, while above these the remainder of the floors were given square windows with transoms and mullions. Another notable feature is the pair of tall chimney stacks that service the fireplaces on both of the end walls. Each of these consists of a bank of five diamond-shaped flues set on a plain base.

BURNCOURT

Burncourt and Kanturk, although both in ruins, offer good examples of the fully developed fortified house. Burncourt in County Tipperary is the younger of the two, judging by the 1641-stone now embedded in the wall of the nearby farmyard. It was built by Sir Richard Everard and consists of a rectangular block about 20 metres long by 7 metres wide, with 5-metre square towers at each corner (Fig. 74). The central block is three storeys over the raised basement, while the corner towers rise to a fourth storey (Fig. 75). These corner towers served a dual purpose. Firstly, they provided extra accommodation. Secondly, they were given small side windows and musket loops (Fig. 76) that provided flanking cover in the event of an attack on the main block. Overhead, the roof line was extremely complex with no fewer than twenty-six gables. The corner towers had four gables each, while the main block had four to the front, four to the rear and a single one at each side.

The basement is lit by small loop-like windows. Above this, the three upper floors have a range of vertically proportioned windows, all aligned horizontally and vertically. This gives an external pattern of window over window and stonework over stonework. Most of the windows are divided into four panes by a single transom and mullion and topped with a hood moulding. The attic windows are similar and set into the gables. The once-fine entrance door, on the south-west elevation, was located slightly off centre and was reached by a short flight of steps. It has elegant moulded jambs, an elliptical head, and a decorated hood moulding, but it is now much damaged. Internally the floors no longer exist, although the damaged fireplaces can be identified. Like Glinsk, the surviving remains of the seven tall chimney stacks can also be identified.

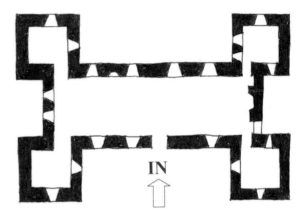

IN

Fig. 74: Ground-floor plan, Burncourt Castle, County Tipperary.

Fig. 75: Burncourt Castle, County Tipperary.

Fig. 76: Musket loop, Burncourt Castle, County Tipperary.

KANTURK CASTLE

Kanturk in County Cork is one of the most impressive examples of a fortified house, although in this case the building was never completed. Dermot McDonagh began work on the house in around 1600, before being ordered to cease work by the British authorities. The order seems to have been complied with, as the roof of the structure was never built.

The plan of Kanturk is similar to Burncourt, with a 27-metre long and 10-metre wide central block with 5-metre square towers at the four corners (Fig. 77). Like Burncourt, the main block is three storeys high over a raised basement, with the corner towers rising a further story (Fig. 78). Also like Burncourt it is impossible to determine the internal room arrangements, but possible to identify the fine fireplaces on a number of floors.

The main difference between Burncourt and Kanturk is in the elevation treatment. In Kanturk the various floor levels are indicated by a projecting string course. Also the windows of the main block are horizontally proportioned and divided into eight panes by transoms and mullions. The corner-tower windows are similar to Burncourt and like Burncourt the towers were given musket loops at ground level. The tower windows are vertically proportioned and divided into four panes by transoms and mullions. The main door on the north side, like Burncourt is in the Renaissance style, and accessed by means of a short flight of steps. It has a semi-circular arch, flanking classical columns and a complex head (Fig. 79). On the opposite side of the building these is a pointed arched door which leads to the basement area.

The roof and parapet of Kanturk was never completed so it is difficult to determine what the builder proposed. Interestingly, a line of projecting corbels stretch around the roofline. Presumably these must have been put in place to carry some form of parapet or crenellations.

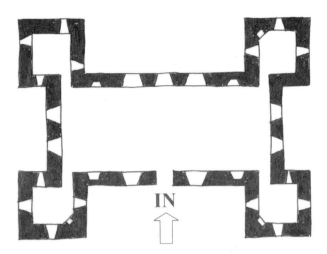

IN

Fig. 77: Ground-
floor plan, Kanturk Castle,
County Cork.

Fig. 78: Kanturk Castle, County Cork.

Fig. 79: Doorway, Kanturk Castle, County Cork.

PORTUMNIA CASTLE

Portumna Castle in County Galway is similar in plan to Kanturk and dates from about 1616. It was built by Richard Burke but was accidentally burnt in 1826. The castle has recently been successfully restored, using eighteenth-century drawings, and is open to the public. It thus presents an image of how other fortified houses of the period looked both internally and externally (Fig. 80). The main rectangular block measures about 30 metres by 20 metres. The corner towers are about 3 metres square although curiously they project outwards far less than Burncourt or Kanturk. The height is similar to Burncourt or Kanturk and consists of a basement, three floors and an attic storey, although the room arrangement seems to have been different.

Internally the main block is divided in a front and rear section by a wide central corridor, built with stone walling. Externally the elevations are completely symmetrical. Each of the corner towers has a central window, while the main block has four larger windows. The tower windows are almost square and each one is divided into two panes by a single mullion. The windows of the main block are taller and are divided into four panes by both a transom and mullion, while the attic windows are dormer types.

The Portumna roof is most complex and consists of three sections: a hipped roof to the front and rear of the block and a gabled roof between the two. All this is partially hidden by the high parapet, which contains a complex arrangement of crenellations, half-round gables and pencil-like finials. The vertical emphases of the corner towers are reduced by a string course set just above the first-floor window level. One of the more notable features of the front elevation is the central-placed doorway. It consists of a semi-circular arch framed by a decorated architrave and head, and topped by a small elliptical window flanked by scrolls and miniature obelisks. Access to the door is provided by a curved flight of steps. Precautions against a possible attack were taken by the inclusion of small round musket loops beside the main door and in the corner towers.

During the reconstruction of the castle, the wooden partitions and room arrangements were recreated. This was based partly on surviving wall marks and on the details in the eighteenth-century drawing. The kitchen and stores are in the basement. The hall and dining rooms are at ground level. The bedrooms are on the first floor and the library and studies are on the third floor. Above this, the staff accommodation was located in the attic storey. Access to the various floors is by means of a reconstructed wooden staircase set in the central corridor.

The castle seems to have had an inner and outer bawn, with the inner bawn extending all around the building. This inner bawn was later revised so that it extended on the entrance, or north, side of the building only. At about the same time the outer bawn was laid out on an axial line immediately north of this. Both spaces were laid out as gardens in geometric patterns. The bawn walls were amended during the eighteen century when the section on the south side of the house were removed and the current gateways and gate lodge were added. Fig. 81 shows the block and the inner bawn, with the garden newly laid out in a geometric pattern – similar to what may have originally existed.

Fig. 80: Portumna Castle, County Galway.

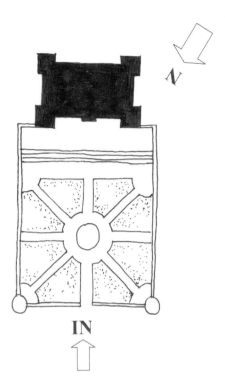

IN

Fig. 81: Plan, castle and inner bawn, Portumna,
County Galway.

The building of the fortified houses and the Plantation castles saw the closing phase of the Irish medieval castle-building movement and after the middle of the seventeenth century few further castles were erected. This did not, however, see the end of military architecture in Ireland, as the eighteenth and nineteenth century saw the construction of a large number of star-shaped forts, shore batteries and Martello towers, particularly around the coastline. These were castle-like in their conception, but totally different in design to their medieval predecessors. For this reason they lie outside the scope of this guide. The nineteenth century also saw the surprising revival of medieval castle-building techniques, when large numbers of pretend, or mock, castles appeared on the Irish landscape.

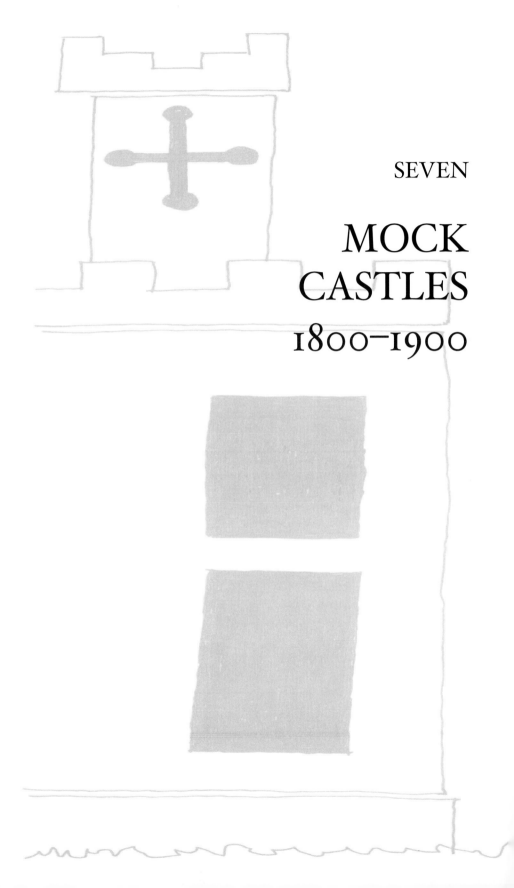

SEVEN

MOCK
CASTLES
1800–1900

THE MOCK CASTLE

One of the surprises of the nineteenth-century Irish landscape is the large number of imitation, or mock, castles to be found in both rural and urban locations. These were built by landowners who chose not to follow the then-current Georgian and Victorian house architecture in favour of a more antique approach. They were not, of course, castles in the true sense, but exercises in antique military forms that often included medieval elements such as walling, battlements, towers, turrets, winding staircases, and loops, as well as Gothic doors and windows. The difference being that, whereas the elements of the true medieval castles had a military and strategic purpose, the same elements in the nineteenth-century mock castles were used solely for decoration and aggrandisements. In fact, so popular did the building of mock castles become that they almost rival the medieval castles in number. Some of the earlier mock castles were eighteenth-century houses that had medieval elements such as battlements and turrets added; while others were completely new structures built on green field sites. A full review of these mock castles lies outside the scope of this guide, but Ardgillan, Dromoland and Glenstall offer typical examples.

Fig. 82: Ardgillan Castle, County Dublin.

ARDGILLAN CASTLE

Ardgillan Castle in County Dublin was an eighteenth-century country house with elaborate bow windows and side wings, which was given a castellated makeover around the beginning of the nineteenth century. The central bow was raised and given the image of a circular wall tower complete with battlements. Below this the rendered walls of the main block and the side wings were given battlements (Fig. 82).

DROMOLAND CASTLE

Dromoland Castle in County Clare was entirely new and built for Sir Edward O'Brien in 1826. The castle consists of a cluster of circular, square and octagonal towers – all varying in height. These are linked together by the main block of the building, which is irregular in height and outline. The towers are crowned with elaborated stepped and projected battlements, while the connecting block was given a more restrained crenulated treatment. The castle was also provided with a range of large windows that reflect its nineteenth-century origins (Fig. 83).

Fig. 83: Dromoland Castle, County Clare.

GLENSTAL ABBEY

Glenstal Abbey, near Limerick City, offers a much larger and more authentic-looking example of a mock castle. It was built for Sir Joseph Barrington in 1837. The layout consists of a large three-storey keep and a massive drum tower, as well as a massive drum-towered gateway (Fig. 84). The tower in particular was given very impressive battlements and the walls were sprinkled with round-headed windows

The difficulty for the visitor to these mock castles is to determine whether it is an original medieval structure or a nineteenth-century copy. Some of the mock castles are so authentic looking that it is difficult to decide on its origin. There are, however, two features in particular that help with the identification of mock castles. The stonework looks crisp and fresh in contrast to the characteristic weathering of true medieval structures, in addition to which, the presence of large windows betrays the work of the nineteenth century.

Some mock castles were exceedingly large indeed and often dwarfed their medieval predecessors in bulk and scale, as the nineteenth-century castle builders required extensive and luxurious accommodation. Even though these clues can provide help in the identification of a mock castle, care is necessary. Some original medieval castles have been subjected to extensive alterations and additions and can easily be mistaken for a mock castle. In the case of Kilkenny Castle, for example, large windows and new elaborate battlements were inserted into an original

Fig. 84: Glenstal Abbey, County Limerick.

medieval structure during the eighteenth and nineteenth century, allowing only the original weathered masonry to reflect the true age of the structure.

Where the mock castle is a ruin, it can be even more difficult to distinguish it from its medieval predecessor. For example, Dromore Castle in County Limerick was built for the Earl of Limerick in about 1867. Here the architect, Edward Goodwin, gave full vent to the medieval military spirit, with massive walls, gatehouses, round towers and battlements. The castle was abandoned after the First World War and all that survives today is a picturesque windswept-looking pile.

EIGHT

GAZETTEER

One of the extraordinary features of the Irish castle-building movement is the number that survive today. Most are in ruinous state but a growing number have been successfully restored. The exact number of castles is uncertain, but undoubtedly the figure extends beyond 3,000. This amounts to an average of about 300 castles per county. Consequently, the visitor to almost any part of country is never far from a castle.

Fig. 85 shows a map of Ireland with the position of the castles mentioned in the text indicated. This is followed by the Gazetteer that offers a selected list of other castles. The list is presented on a county by county basis to assist those who wish to view a range of castles. Within this grouping, the castles are arranged by historical types, for ease of identification. This, it is hoped, will help the visitor to recognise and enjoy the individual castles. The list is not of course conclusive; such a list would run into thousands of examples and would be well beyond the scope of this guide. Rather, the list includes castles that are recognisably of their type and are prominently located on the landscape. It should, however, be remembered that most castles were altered or extended in the years following their formative building phase. Consequently, some display features are characteristic of a number of different historic periods. Malahide Castle in County Dublin and Carbury Castle in County Kildare, for example, have elements that date from the thirteenth, sixteenth, seventeenth, eighteenth and nineteenth centuries. Generally these phases are recognisable. However, it is worth remembering that the building history of some castles can be difficult to disentangle and understand.

A number of the major Irish castles have been very successfully restored and furnished, and are particularly worth visiting. These give an accurate impression of the spatial and living conditions enjoyed by the occupants and include:

Carrickfergus, County Antrim
Cahir, County Tipperary
King John's Castle, Limerick
Bunratty, County Clare
Carrick-on-Suir, County Tipperary
Portumna, County Galway

All of these date from the Anglo-Norman period, except for Bunratty which dates from the fifteenth century; as well as Carick-on-Suir, Park's and Portumna which date from the late sixteenth and early seventeenth century. The timing of any visit, however, must be chosen with care as some of these are not open during the winter months.

Many of the examples listed in the Gazetteer are in public ownership and so are open to visitors, while a great many others are in private ownership. Others can be very difficult to find. Clara in County Kilkenny, Coolhull in County Wexford and Ballynahow in County Tiperary, for instance, are located within existing farmyards and are difficult to locate without the benefit

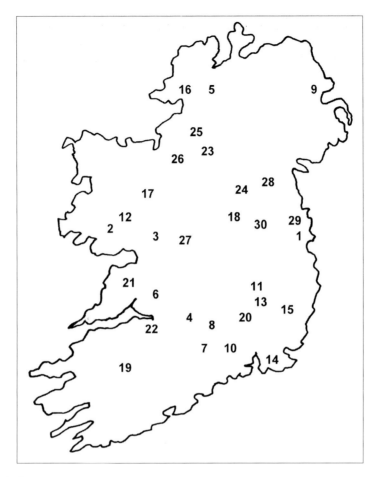

Fig. 85: Castles in the text.

1. Ashtown, County Dublin
2. Aughnanure, County Galway
3. Athenry, County Galway
4. Ballynahow, County Tipperary
5. Brackfield, County Derry
6. Bunratty, County Clare
7. Burncourt, County Tipperary
8. Cahir, County Tipperary
9. Carrickfergus, County Antrim
10. Carrick-on-Suir, County Tipperary
11. Carlow, County Carlow
12. Castle Kirk, County Galway
13. Clara, County Kilkenny
14. Coole Hull, County Wexford
15. Ferns, County Wexford
16. Donegal, County Donegal
17. Glinsk, County Galway
18. Granard, County Longford
19. Kanturk, County Cork
20. Kilkenny, County Kilkenny
21. Leamaneh, County Clare
22. Limerick, County Limerick
23. Monea, County Fermanagh
24. Nobber, County Meath
25. Tully, County Fermanagh
26. Park's Castle, County Leitrim
27. Portumna, County Galway
28. Roodstown, County Louth
29. Swords, County Dublin
30. Trim, County Meath

of detailed local maps. Where castles are in private ownership, permission to visit the site must be secured from the owner. In most cases this is generously granted, but there are occasions where access can be withheld for a range of security and privacy reasons. Such refusals are rare, but must be respected. In any event, enjoy the experience, do not cause damage or leave litter, and remember to close all gates.

ULSTER

COUNTY ANTRIM
Motte-and-Baileys: Ballywalter, Harryville
Anglo-Norman Castles: Carrickfergus, Dunluce
Tower Houses: Olderfleet
Plantation Castles: Dalway's Bawn, Kilbane, Ballygally

COUNTY ARMAGH
Fortified Houses: Moyry

COUNTY CAVAN
Anglo-Norman Castles: Clogh Oughter

COUNTY DERRY
Motte-and-Baileys: Mill Loughan
Plantation Castles: Bellaghy, Brackfield

COUNTY DONEGAL
Anglo-Norman Castles: Buncrana, Greencastle
Tower Houses: Doe
Fortified Houses: Burt, Donegal, Raphoe

COUNTY DOWN
Motte-and-Baileys: Clough, Duneight, Dromore Holywood, Mound, Shandon Park,
Anglo-Norman Castles: Dundrum, Greencastle
Tower Houses: Ardglass, Audley's Castle, Kilclief, Portaferry, Narrow Water
Plantation Castles: Killyleagh

COUNTY FERMAMAGH
Plantation Castles: Castle Archdale, Aghalahane, Castle Balfour, Enniskillen (Fig. 86)
Monea, Tully

Fig. 86: Enniskillen Castle, Enniskillen, County Fermanagh.

COUNTY MONAGHAN
Motte-and-Baileys: Cloyne, Mannan
Anglo-Norman Castles: Donaghmoyne

COUNTY TYRONE
Anglo-Norman Castles: Harry Avery's Castle
Plantation Castles: Benburb, Castle Caulfield, Mountjoy, Roughan

LEINSTER

COUNTY CARLOW
Motte-and-Baileys: St Mullins
Anglo-Norman Castles: Ballyloughan, Ballymoon, Carlow Town
Tower Houses: Leighlinbridge

COUNTY DUBLIN (NORTH)
Motte-and-Baileys: Knocksedan, Malahide
Anglo-Norman Castles: Howth, Malahide, Swords
Tower Houses: Dunabate, Dunsoghley, Phoenix Park
Fortified Houses: Lambay Island

COUNTY DUBLIN (SOUTH)
Anglo-Norman Castles: Dublin Castle, Dalkey
Tower Houses: Clondalkin, Dalkey (Fig. 87), Drimnagh, Monkstown
Fortified Houses: Rathfarnham

COUNTY KILDARE
Motte-and-Baileys: Ardscull, Cloncurry, Mainham, Naas, Old Connell
Anglo-Norman Castles: Leixlip, Maynooth, Rathcoffey
Tower Houses: Grange, Kilteel, Naas
Fortified Houses: Carbury

COUNTY KILKENNY
Motte-and-Baileys: Ardscull, Callen
Anglo-Norman Castles: Grannagh, Granny, Grenan, Kilkenny City
Tower Houses: Balief, Burnchurch, Clara, Granagh

COUNTY LAOIS
Motte-and-Baileys: Aghaboe
Anglo-Norman Castles: Dunamase, Lea

Fig. 87: Tower House, Dalkey, County Dublin.

COUNTY LONGFORD
Motte-and-Baileys: Granard

COUNTY LOUTH
Motte-and-Baileys: Drogheda, Dun Dealgan, Greenmount
Anglo-Norman Castles: Carlingford, Castleroche
Tower Houses: Ardee (Fig. 88), Carlingford, Roodstown, Termonfeckin

COUNTY MEATH
Motte-and-Baileys: Clonard, Milltown, Nobber
Anglo-Norman Castles: Dunmoe, Trim
Tower Houses: Donore
Plantation Castles: Robertstown
Fortified Houses: Athlumney

COUNTY OFFALLY
Motte-and-Baileys: Clonmacnois, Leap
Anglo-Norman Castles: Birr
Tower Houses: Clonony
Fortified Houses: Ballycowan

COUNTY WESTMEATH
Motte-and-Baileys: Castletown Geoghegan, Glebe, Moate, Tonashammer
Anglo-Norman Castles: Athlone (Fig. 89), Delvin
Tower Houses: Tyrrellspass

COUNTY WEXFORD
Motte-and-Baileys: Old Ross
Anglo-Norman Castles: Coolhull, Enniscorthy, Ferns, Rathumney
Tower Houses: Ballyhack, Carnew, Clonmines, Rathmacknee, Slade

COUNTY WICKLOW
Motte-and-Baileys: Castlekevin, Castleruddery Lower, Donore, Newcastle, Oldcourt, Wicklow Town
Anglo-Norman Castles: Arklow Castle, Wicklow Town
Tower Houses: Blessington, Carnew, Kiltimon, Kindlestown, Oldcourt, Threecastles
Fortified Houses: Dunganstown

Fig. 88: Tower House, Ardee, County Louth.

Fig. 89: Athlone Castle, County Westmeath.

MUNSTER

COUNTY CLARE
Tower Houses: Bunratty, Carrigaholt, Corrafin, Dysert–O'Dea, Gleninagh, Knappogue, Newtown (Fig. 90), Quinn
Fortified Houses: Gleninagh, Leamaneh

COUNTY CORK
Anglo-Norman Castles: Glanworth, Castle Mora, Kilbolane, Liscarroll
Tower Houses: Blarney Ballynacarriga, Barryscourt, Ballynamona, Carrigaphooca, Conna, Drishane, Kinsale, Kilcolman, Kinsale
Fortified Houses: Coppinger's Court, Drumaneen, Ightermurragh, Kanturk, Mallow, Monkstown, Mountlong

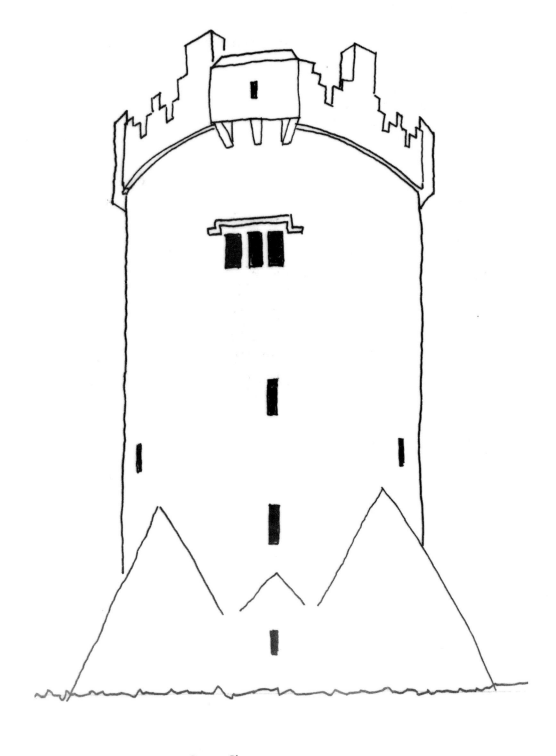

Fig. 90: Tower House, Newtown, County Clare.

COUNTY KERRY
Anglo-Norman Castles: Aghadoe, Ballycarbery, Carrigafoyle
Tower Houses: Ballymalis, Carrigafoyle, Gallarus, Killarney, Ratinnane, Listowel, Ross

COUNTY LIMERICK
Motte-and-Baileys: Shanid
Anglo-Norman Castles: Adare, Askeaton, Carrigogunnell, Limerick City, Newcastle West
Tower Houses: Castle Matrix, Ballingarry, Ballygrennan, Bouchier's Castle, Bunratty, Glenquin, Kilmallock, Rockstown

COUNTY TIPPERARY
Motte-and-Baileys: Knockgraffon, Moatquarter
Anglo-Norman Castles: Cahir, Castlegrace, Nenagh, Roscrea (Fig. 91), Terryglass
Tower Houses: Ballynahow, Fethard, Grallagh, Kilcash, Knockkelly, Lakeen, Loughmoe, Two-Mile-Borris
Fortified Houses: Borrisokane, Burncourt, Carrick-on-Suir, Killenure, Knockkelly, Lehinch, Loughmoe

COUNTY WATERFORD
Anglo-Norman Castles: Dungarvan, Reginald's Tower

CONNAUGHT

COUNTY GALWAY
Anglo-Norman Castles: Athenry, Castletown, Dunmore, Kiltartan
Tower Houses: Ardmullivan, Aughnanure, Ballaghmore, Ballylee, Castlegrove, Creagh, Derryhivenny, Drumharsna, Dungory, Dunguaire, Dunmore, Fertagar, Fiddaun, Galway Headford, Inisheer, Isert Kelly, Kinvara, Loughrea.
Plantation Castles: Inishmore
Fortified Houses: Glinsk, Portumna

COUNTY LEITRIM
Plantation Castles: Parke's Castle
Tower Houses: Ballagharahin, Ballaghmore

COUNTY MAYO
Anglo-Norman Castles: Ballylahan, Castlekirk, Shrule
Tower Houses: Aghalard, Carrickkildavnet, Castlecarra, Kinlough, Rockfleet
Fortified Houses: Deel

Fig. 91: Gatehouse, Roscrea Castle, County Tipperary.

Fig. 92: Roscommon Castle, County Roscommon.

COUNTY ROSCOMMON
Anglo-Norman Castles: Ballintober, Roscommon Town (Fig. 92), Rinndown, Templemore

COUNTY SLIGO
Anglo-Norman Castles: Ballymote, Temple House
Plantation Castles: Ballinafad
Fortified Houses: Ardtermon, Castlebaldwin

Leabharlanna Poibli Chathair Bhaile Átha Cliath
Dublin City Public Libraries